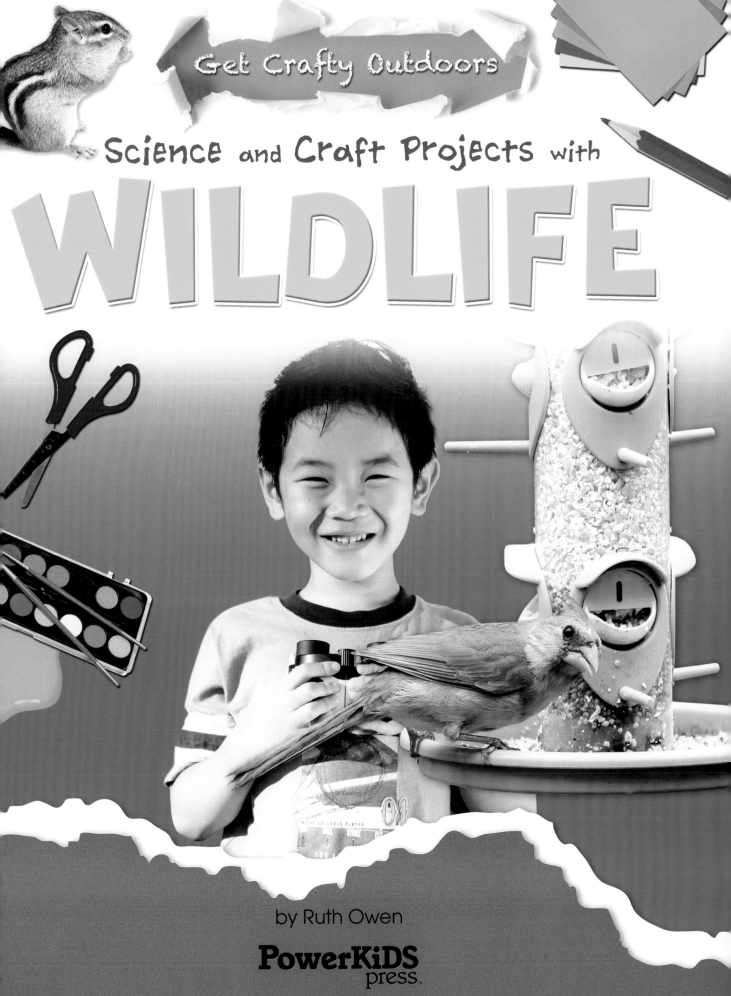

Get Crafty Outdoors

Science and Craft Projects with

WILDLIFE

by Ruth Owen

PowerKiDS press

New York

Published in 2013 by The Rosen Publishing Group, Inc.
29 East 21st Street, New York, NY 10010

Produced for Rosen by Ruby Tuesday Books Ltd
Editor for Ruby Tuesday Books Ltd: Mark J. Sachner
US Editor: Sara Antill
Designer: Emma Randall
Consultant: Suzy Gazlay

Photo Credits:
Cover, 1, 4–5, 6 (bottom), 7, 8, 10–11, 14–15, 18–19, 20, 21 (top), 22–23, 26–27 © Shutterstock; 6 (top) © FLPA; 9, 12–13, 16–17, 21 (center), 21 (bottom), 24–25, 27 (bottom), 28–29 © Ruby Tuesday Books Ltd.

Library of Congress Cataloging-in-Publication Data

Owen, Ruth, 1967–
 Science and craft projects with wildlife / by Ruth Owen.
     p. cm. — (Get crafty outdoors)
 Includes index.
 ISBN 978-1-4777-0243-7 (library binding) — ISBN 978-1-4777-0249-9 (pbk.) — ISBN 978-1-4777-0250-5 (6-pack)
 1. Animals—Juvenile literature. 2. Nature study—Juvenile literature. 3. Handicraft—Juvenile literature. I. Title.
 QL49.O836 2013
 745.592—dc23

                              2012026381

Manufactured in the United States of America

CPSIA Compliance Information: Batch #W13PK7: For Further Information contact Rosen Publishing, New York, New York at 1-800-237-9932

Contents

Wild Neighbors

When you look outside your window, do you see houses, stores, and cars? Do you see trees and fields instead? This is your neighborhood. It's probably also the neighborhood of many wild animals.

A squirrel sits in a backyard flowerpot.

Birds, frogs, chipmunks, squirrels, raccoons, or foxes may be living in your backyard or in a nearby park. If you live in the country, you might have deer or coyotes as **wildlife** neighbors.

A duck and ducklings swim in the pond in a park.

This book is all about the wild animals that live in our towns, cities, and countrysides. You will find out how they survive and raise their young. You will also get the chance to make some cool wildlife crafts!

Animal Habitats

The area where an animal lives is called its **habitat**. A habitat might be as large as a forest or as small as a garden pond. In its habitat, an animal must be able to find water and food. It also needs a safe home where it can raise its young, find shelter from weather, and hide from enemies.

Birds, Nests, Eggs, and Chicks

Spring and summer are the seasons when most wild birds have their young. At this time of year, you might see birds collecting materials to build nests where they will lay their eggs.

nest material

robin

After a male and female robin **mate**, the female builds a nest in a tree or thick bush. She makes the nest from twigs and grass. She might also use feathers and pieces of paper trash.

nest

robin egg

The nest is a safe place for the robin to lay her eggs. Then she sits on the eggs to keep them warm.

robin chicks

nest

After about 14 days, the robin chicks hatch from the eggs. They live in the nest until they are two weeks old and are strong enough to fly.

Mud Nests

Different kinds of birds build different types of nests. Swallows collect mud in their beaks from the edges of ponds and streams. Then they use the mud to build their nests.

swallow chick

mud nest

Build a Bird's Nest

Try building a bird's nest and find out just how hard wild birds have to work!

You will need:

- A bag for collecting nesting material
- Twigs
- Dry grass
- Moss
- Leaves
- Pieces of paper or cardboard trash
- Feathers
- Garden soil and water to make mud
- Sheets of newspaper

Get Crafty:

1 Collect materials to build a nest from your backyard, schoolyard, or a park.

dry grass

twigs

moss

dry leaves

feathers

paper or cardboard trash

2 Remember, you can only use materials that you find in the wild. Birds can't visit a craft store to buy string or tape!

3 Place sheets of newspaper on a table or countertop and lay out all the materials you have found.

4 Use the twigs to make a framework for the nest. Try weaving them together to make a bowl shape.

5 Use grass, moss, and feathers to pad out the inside of the nest. If you wish, you can mix soil and water to make mud. Smear the mud onto the nest and use it like glue to hold the other nest materials together.

6 When you have finished making your nest, ask an adult to help you place it in a tree or bush—just like a real bird's nest!

7 Always wash your hands with hot water and soap after working with materials you find outdoors.

Busy Birds

Did you find it difficult or easy to build a nest? Remember, you were able to use your hands. A bird must build its nest using its beak and feet. Also, a bird cannot collect all its nest materials at once. It has to make hundreds of journeys to collect the materials it needs.

Raccoon Neighbors

Many wild mammals, such as raccoons and squirrels, have their young in spring.

house roof

adult raccoon

Female raccoons give birth to their cubs, or kits, in a safe home called a den. Raccoons build dens in holes in trees. Sometimes they make dens in spaces under the roofs of houses.

The mother raccoon feeds the cubs with milk from her body.

The cubs stay in the den until they are about eight weeks old.

tree den

raccoon cubs

This raccoon cub is climbing a tree.

When the cubs leave the den, they learn how to climb trees.

The mother raccoon teaches the cubs how to find food such as fruit, plants, eggs, and **insects**.

This raccoon cub is eating a plant.

Smart Food Thieves

Raccoons sometimes steal dog or cat food from the porches of houses. They also look in garbage cans to find leftover human food.

Make a Raccoon Mask

Raccoons have black fur on their faces that looks like a mask. Follow the instructions here to make your own fantastic raccoon mask.

You will need:

- A paper plate
- Gray paint
- A paintbrush
- Scissors
- A piece of cardboard
- Glue
- Black felt
- Pink felt
- A wooden stick or tongue depressor
- 6 white drinking straws
- Tape
- Chalk
- An adult to help with cutting

Get Crafty:

 Paint the paper plate gray.

Ask an adult to help you cut two triangles from the cardboard to make ears. Paint the ears gray. When the paint is dry, glue the ears to the paper plate.

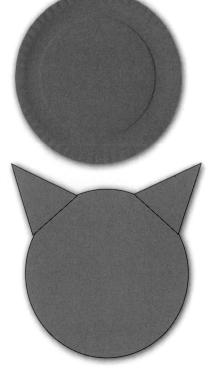

 Cut two small triangles from the black felt and glue these to the ears. Make sure an adult helps you cut the felt shapes for your mask.

3 Cut an oval shape in the black felt to make the raccoon's eye mask. The oval must be as wide as the paper plate. Then cut a second thinner oval shape from the black felt. Glue the shapes to the plate.

4 Cut a triangle from the black felt to make the raccoon's nose. Cut a semicircle shape from the pink felt to make a tongue. Glue these two pieces onto the paper plate.

5 Tape the wooden stick to the back of the mask.

6 Glue three straws to each side of the raccoon's face to make whiskers.

7 Finally, hold the mask up to your face. Ask an adult to gently make chalk marks on the mask where your eyes are. Then ask the adult to cut two eye holes in the mask with sharp scissors or a craft knife.

From Tadpoles to Frogs

If you look into a pond or lake in spring, you might see a big glob of frog eggs.

female frog

frog eggs

After mating, a female frog lays thousands of eggs in water. Each tiny black egg is inside a blob of see-through jelly.

jelly

egg

A baby frog called a tadpole hatches from each egg. The tadpoles have long tails and no legs. They look more like fish than frogs.

tadpole

head

tail

The tadpoles go through lots of changes. First they grow back legs. Then they grow front legs. Their tails get shorter, too.

back leg

short tail

back leg   front leg

Finally, the tadpoles' tails disappear and they become adult frogs!

adult frog

How Do Tadpoles Breathe?

A frog uses its **lungs** to breathe **oxygen** from the air, like you. A tadpole can only breathe underwater, like a fish. It uses body parts called **gills** to take oxygen out of the water. As it changes into a frog, a tadpole grows lungs for breathing air.

Frog Life Cycle Collage

The stages of an animal's life are called a life cycle. In the first stage of a frog's life, a female frog lays eggs. Tadpoles hatch from the eggs and grow into frogs. The frogs mate and produce more eggs, and the cycle begins again. In this collage, you can show how a frog's life cycle is like a circle.

You will need:

- A large piece of cardboard
- Scissors
- Aluminum foil
- Green construction paper, felt, or scraps of fabric.
- White construction paper
- 3 black buttons
- A piece of red or pink ribbon or string

- Colorful buttons to make spots
- Glue
- Bubble wrap
- Black marker
- Brown paper
- Red paper
- An adult to be your teammate and to help with cutting

Get Crafty:

1 Ask an adult to help you cut the large piece of cardboard into a circle to make a pond background. Cover the cardboard circle with aluminum foil.

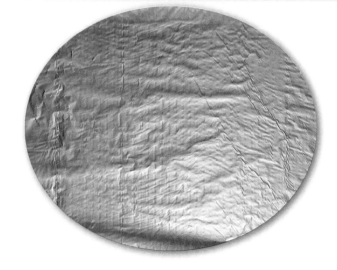

To make the frog's head and body, cut two circles from green construction paper, felt, or fabric. Ask an adult to help you with the cutting.

3 Draw the frog's feet onto the green paper or fabric and cut them out.

4 Cut two small circles from the white construction paper.

5 Now glue all the frog pieces onto the pond. Add two black buttons to the frog's eyes and a ribbon mouth. You can glue on extra buttons to give your frog spotty skin.

6 Glue some bubble wrap to the pond. Use the marker to add black dots for eggs.

7 To make the tadpole, cut an oval from the brown paper. Cut a long shape to make the tadpole's tail. Glue the tadpole pieces onto the pond. Add a black button eye.

8 Add paper arrows to the frog life cycle.

Hungry Birds

Wild birds spend hours every day looking for food and eating.

Some birds, such as waxwings, mainly eat **seeds**, berries, and fruit.

waxwing

berries

Other birds, such as robins, eat grasshoppers, caterpillars, and other insects. They also eat small animals such as worms.

robin

worms

In winter it can be difficult for wild birds to find enough food. Most plants do not produce seeds or fruit in winter. Also, there are few insects around.

People can help wild birds in winter by giving them food. Nuts, sunflower seeds, and food scraps can be placed on a bird table. Bird feeders filled with seeds can be hung in trees.

bird feeder

cardinal

Be a Bird Watcher

Watch the birds in your garden, backyard, or nearby park.
Try to spot the following:
- **A bird eating seeds or berries from a plant.**
- **A bird with a worm in its beak.**
- **A bird looking under leaves to find insects.**
- **A bird drinking water from a pond, puddle, or birdbath.**

Make a Bird Feeder

You can help the wild birds that live near you by making a pinecone bird feeder for them to visit in the winter.

You will need:

- Large pinecone with open scales
- Vegetable shortening
- Wild birdseed (from a pet store)
- Other ingredients, which may include crushed fresh peanuts (not roasted or salted), stale bread, cake, cookie crumbs, cheese crumbs, or dried fruit.

- A measuring cup
- A spoon
- A plate
- 4 feet (1.2 m) of string
- An adult teammate to help you go pinecone gathering and help you tie your bird feeder to a tree branch.

Get Crafty:

1 You can visit a park or forest where there are pine trees to find pinecones. It's also possible to buy pinecones from craft stores.

2 Tie one end of the string around the top of the pinecone.

open scales

pinecone

3 Pour one cup of wild birdseed and the other ingredients onto the plate.

wild birdseed

dried fruit

cookie crumbs

4 Spread lots of shortening over the pinecone with the spoon.

5 Roll the shortening-covered pinecone in the seeds and other ingredients. Use the spoon to push lots of seed and shortening between the pinecone's scales. Try to pack as many goodies onto the pinecone as possible!

6 Ask an adult to help you tie the pinecone outside. A tree branch or a porch is a good place. Make sure you choose a place where cats cannot pounce on the birds as they feed.

7 Keep watch for birds visiting your feeder!

Storing Food for Winter

squirrel

In winter, it can be difficult for wild mammals, such as squirrels and chipmunks, to find enough food to eat.

In the fall, squirrels collect acorns that fall from oak trees.

acorns

They bury the acorns in the ground. Then, when there is no food around in winter, they dig up their buried food.

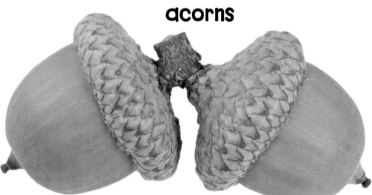

Chipmunks live in underground homes called burrows.

hole leading to burrow

chipmunk

During the fall, a chipmunk collects thousands of nuts and seeds. It stores this food in its burrow.

Then the chipmunk spends the cold winter months sleeping in its burrow. If it gets hungry, it eats some of its stored food.

Chubby Chipmunk Cheeks

Chipmunks carry nuts and seeds in a **pouch** in each of their cheeks. A chipmunk can stuff about 60 sunflower seeds into each cheek pouch!

cheek filled with food

Make Chipmunk Storage Jars

Just like a chipmunk, you can store small toys, coins, or delicious snack foods such as nuts and sunflower seeds in these great chipmunk storage jars.

You will need:

- Clean, empty jars with lids
- Glue
- Scissors
- Orange or dark brown felt
- Pale brown or yellow felt
- White felt
- Black felt
- Pink felt
- An adult to be your teammate and to help with cutting

Get Crafty:

1 You can use pickle, mayonnaise, or jam jars to make your storage jars.

2 Take the lid off a jar and cover the outside of the lid with glue. Put glue around the sides of the lid, too.

3 Lay the lid glue side down on a piece of orange felt that is slightly larger than the lid. Press down firmly. Then fold up the felt so that it sticks to the sides of the lid.

4 Ask an adult to trim off any spare felt so the whole lid is neatly covered with felt. You now have your chipmunk's face.

5 Cut these shapes from the orange, pale brown, black, white, and pink felt. Remember, the shapes must fit onto the lid, or face.

ears

eye patches

eyes

cheek

cheek

nose

teeth

6 Now glue the shapes onto the face. First, stick on the ears, eye patches, eyes, and teeth.

7 Then glue on the two cheeks. Finally, glue on the nose.

8 Allow the glue to dry. Your storage jar is ready to fill with goodies!

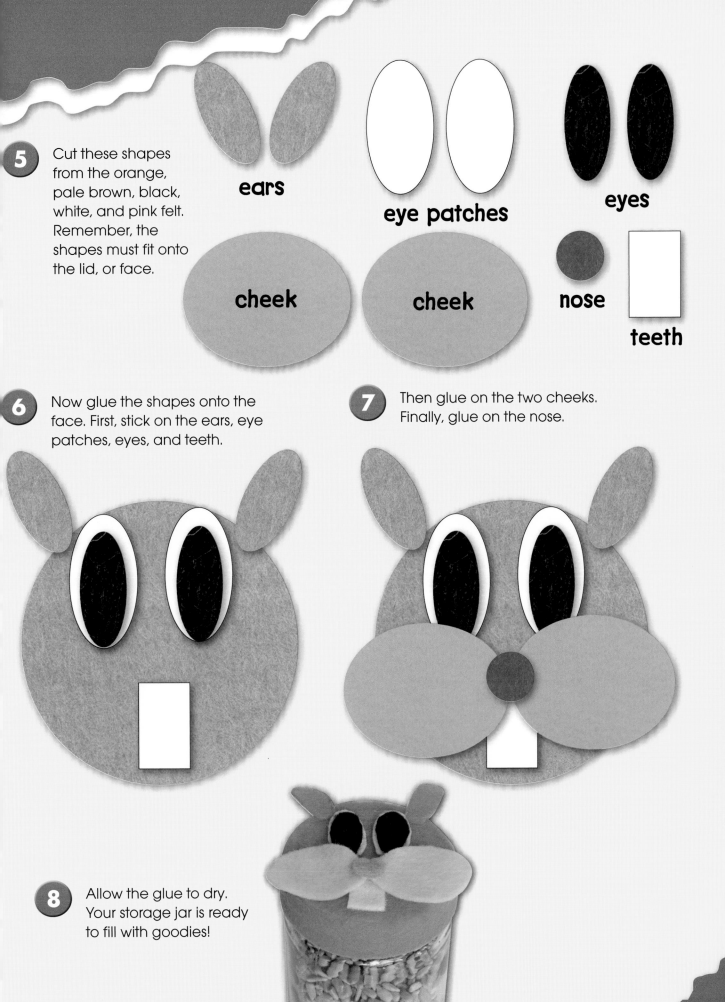

Tracking Wildlife

One way to find out what animals live in your neighborhood is to look for tracks, or footprints.

Animal tracks can show you what places an animal vistted. You might even be able to follow the tracks to find out where the animal went next!

Look for tracks in mud or snow.

You might see muddy footprints on the hood of a car.

Animals may leave tracks in sand at a playground.

You can take photographs of the tracks you spot. Before you take the photograph, put a dime next to the track. This will show the real-life size of the footprint.

bird tracks

Get Tracking

squirrel

raccoon

bear

dog

cat

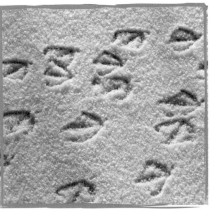

duck

Making Tracks

On a dry day, try sprinkling a layer of flour on a flat surface in your garden or schoolyard. Then place a plate of food in the center. See page 20 for ideas of which foods to use. The next day, check the flour for tracks to see if birds or other animals have visited the food.

Make Animal Track Models

If you find an animal footprint in sand or dried mud, you can make a cast, or model, of the footprint to keep! You can also make your own tracks in modeling clay and then make casts of them.

You will need:

- Plaster of Paris
- Water
- A bowl
- A spoon for mixing
- A strip of cardboard about 18 inches (46 cm) long and 1 inch (2.5 cm) wide
- A paperclip
- Modeling clay if you are making your own tracks

Get Crafty:

1 Find a track or make one in modeling clay.

Using the cardboard strip and paperclip, make a little collar, or wall, around the track.

 You will need to make enough plaster mix to fill the collar. Put some plaster of Paris into the bowl and start adding water.

 Stir the mixture to remove any lumps. The mixture should be the thickness of pancake batter. Keep adding plaster or water until the mix is right.

5 Start gently pouring the mix into the collar to the side of the print. Let the mix slowly run into the print so it doesn't damage its shape. Then fill the rest of the area inside the collar with mix.

6 The plaster should set hard in about 30 minutes. Gently touch the plaster to find out if it is dry and hard. If it still feels soft, leave it for another 10 minutes and then try again.

7 When the plaster is hard and dry, remove the collar. Very carefully lift up the model using two hands on opposite sides of the model. On the underside of the model will be a cast of the footprint!

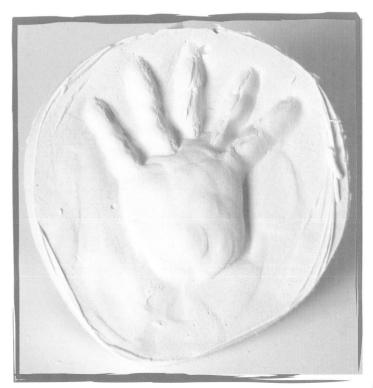

8 Allow the cast to dry out for three or four more days before cleaning or painting it.

9 If you need to clean dirt or sand from the model, hold it under a slow-flowing tap. Let the water gently wash off the dirt. When the model has dried out again, you can paint it if you wish.

Glossary

gills (GILZ)
Body parts that some water animals, such as fish and tadpoles, use for breathing.

habitat (HA-buh-tat)
The place where an animal or plant normally lives. A habitat may be a backyard, a forest, the ocean, or a pond in a park.

insect (IN-sekt)
A small animal with six legs, a body in three parts, and a hard outer shell, called an exoskeleton.

lungs (LUNGZ)
Body parts that humans and other animals use for breathing air.

mammal (MA-mul)
A warm-blooded animal that has a backbone and usually has hair. Mammals give birth to live babies and feed them milk from their bodies.

mate (MAYT)
When a male and female come together to produce young.

oxygen (OK-sih-jen)
A gas in the air that is needed by humans and other animals for breathing.

pouch (POWCH)
A body part that's a little like a pocket.

seed (SEED)
A part of a plant that contains all the material needed to grow a new plant.

wildlife (WYLD-lyf)
Animals that live wild in their natural habitat and are not pets, farm animals, or zoo animals.

Websites

Due to the changing nature of Internet links, PowerKids Press has developed an online list of websites related to the subject of this book. This site is updated regularly. Please use this link to access the list:
www.powerkidslinks.com/gco/wild/

Read More

Ryall, Jeanette. *Nature Art*. Awesome Art. New York: Windmill Books, 2013.

Schwarz, Renee. *Birdfeeders*. Kids Can Do It. Tonawanda, NY: Kids Can Press, 2005.

Thompson, Ruth. *A Frog's Life Cycle*. Let's Look at Life Cycles. New York: PowerKids Press, 2010.

Index